I0832224

VANDAL

(poems of disentanglement)

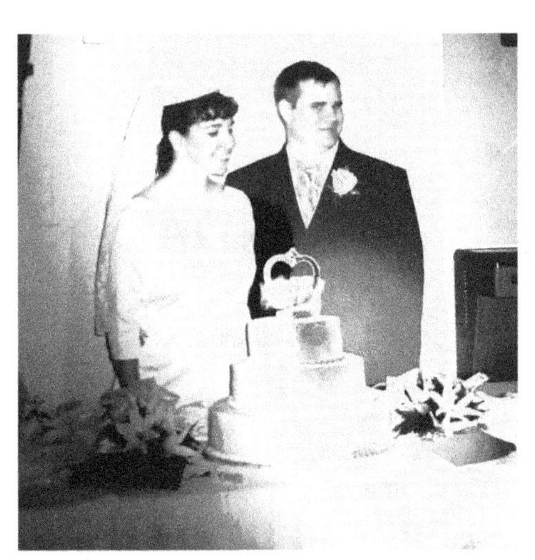

VANDAL

(disentanglement)

"Life is one continuous Hallucinism. Chaos reigns."

—-Angela Yuriko Smith

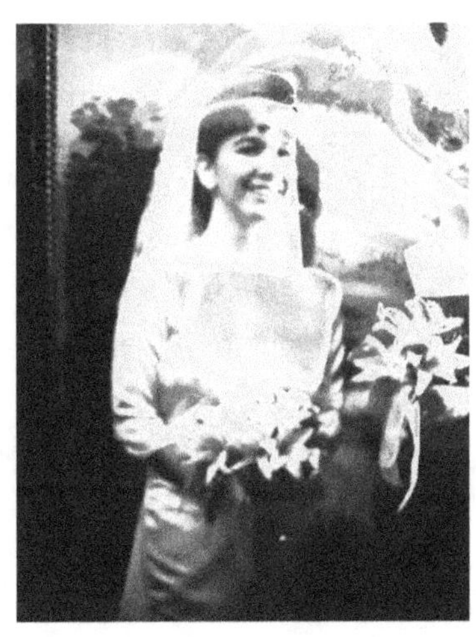

...

Vandal No. 1

for what have I primed myself
in these reveries since age 14?
Every wakeful moment riding in a car
in darkness of movie house
daydreaming in lectures
falling into sleep
then, then and then and then:
rocked in tender splendor of any conjured love?
My smorgasbord? Singers in their revolving
chapters.
When it came to life—
MaNiFeSTed—
A Feast—
I could not defend myself.

Vandal No. 2

numbskull
you wished to defend yourself?
lusciously
numb-of-skull
you wished no such thing.
The river is never mindful
and far less so,
this time,
its traveler.

...

Vandal No. 3

I, vandal, cry poetry!
(invoking Special Poetical Dispensation)

Here materializes poetry.
I must have it.
Give it me.
These threaded jewels.
I, poet, am obligated
to swig it as miracle
as tingling spring wine.
Radiant tonic. An uncanny charm.

Before:
starved.
staunchly horrid.
The flourishing godless of DESIRE
FOR MORE.
For visibility to end
the maniac's laughter.

When the plate returned to me,
empty,
staunch horridness did flourish
—and how—

until everything burned glazed glorious
in cinders
at the end.

Vandal No. 4

River of Melancholy
River forgets
Forgets to be properly self-scandalized
Forgets to be Christianly sanitized
anesthetized
drugged in the drug of the outdated shuddering rule
and why do I uphold my scandal?
My selfish rude?
My forfeit of the gravestone reward
inscribed "AN UNSELFISH LIFE"?

AT REST, they all say,
sensing my decades of flail
and flailing on I go

Yes, Vandal.

But this sin stops the bleeding.
This sin muzzles the flailing.
Coiled now in comfort.
Grief all but shucked.
There now. Warmed
and Hushed.

...

Vandal No. 5

Ahh, dear father
my graveyard
tell me how to be

testifying as you do
with your granite faces...

POET says one.
No further instruction.
I turn to the One I See.
I turn to the
Grocery.
Bearded one, fearless.
Tell me how to be.

I seek confirmation
huddled in shag-carpet
babysitting basement of old,
ceiling-sparkled,
little girls asleep upstairs and
fearless of thunderstorms,
and I knowing nothing but angel-glow
for all guitarists out of reach
out of question
never questioned
perfect in hope and delirious.

Vandal No. 6

Mother
Doomed Mother

Whom will you wound and when?
Whom will you wound
again?
You
who used to mother
in fashion sort of grand?
(sometimes)

I claim the devil's milk jug

to fill with maple serenity (costly)
(cracked in three upon arrival)

…

Vandal No. 7

Fast. Pray amid the flinging waves and waterspouts.

Abstain from food.
Devote yourself to prayer
saying?
Don't take him away, Lord.
I want him near me.
I want his magnetic,
profoundly sad eyes ~
to turn them in my hands
like luminous marbles clacking,
puddling, pale as dawn,
to hold them high
under jellyfish sky
of full June Strawberry Moon.

I want him near me
to watch him die
in agony of smoke and mouth cancer?
To collect his lung-vomit in my gown
To collect his ancient glittering eyes
To stow them in my puzzle box?
To dash them on the pavement?
Punished. Obliterated, both.
Deserved deserved.

(so say the all-knowing children)

By summer’s end I will have aged
gaunt and boneless
shrunken-eyed and
hunched for my sins.

…

Vandal No. 8

Fast. Pray amid the cyclones and chaos.

By summer's end I will have flung a number of clay bowls,
crooked,
on the chaos-wheel
and dipped them in jewel-glazes
to send him away, full-handed.
To send them both upon
their respective journeys
Elsewhere
Burdened under clay bowls
laden with pumpkin seeds and black radishes.

Abstain from food.
Devote yourself to prayer.
Saying saying saying….

My child who was my child
my dearest longing
my one true knowing,
second only to Christ
in my nearest most exquisite joy

let him hate me now.
Oh, he will. I have traded him
for chaos poetry
for the keys to the love songs
for a taste of nicotine-teeth giddy laughter
heady aftershave
a solid form. To be real again,
existent.

I throw my bowls
and knit my hats
and commandeer
the wheel of chaos
and drive this vessel
over the edge
and into the thundering sea.

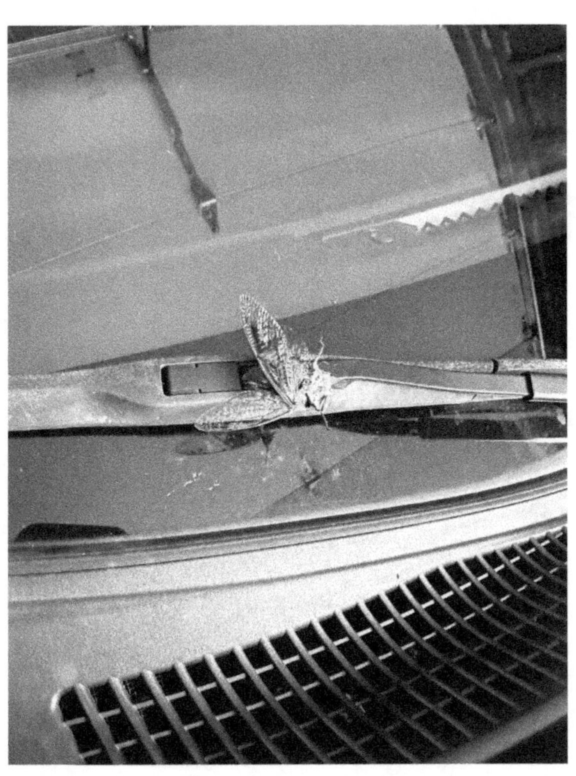

...

Vandal No. 9

The hinged photographs
of the in-laws on the fireplace mantle
are still the truth at current.

The in-laws on the mantle
are currently the 'in' truth.

Stare at the truth of a
mundane & superior current.
Stare at the truth,
postponing transgression &
offense.

Dance the age-old reel
of poet –   twined –
with twentieth-century female:
Dare I eat the donut and take up space?
Dare I miss the opportunity to gorge
on the tartlets of LIFE?
Jellyroll me.

Snuggle me unto the tongues that cluck.

Vandal 10

We've known each other long years
and how close have I come to
confiding in you
about the other guy?
The tornado that hit his bedroom
in Sedalia when he was five.
Sassy banter with friend
regarding a carved flute
and his fragrance of baby detergent.
Two of the four songs he wrote to me.
Only just skirting
the borderline-unforgivable, the weird and the rude.

...

Vandal 11

Mayheming I ran
untrammeled! defiant!
into the orbit of the battered tooth enamel

freely into anxiety’s orchard
of weeping, aromatic peaches
–skin smooth, immaculate,
smoke-addled.
Caffeinated.
Hot dog poisoned.
Cancer candidate.

Mayhemmed in, I am
trammeled of music.
Drunk with poetry.
Cemented in blessing.

Vandal 12

we chose dahlias
and they blazed with health,
flooding the dirt path
with impudent blooms

declaring good omens,
smiling on our marigolds,
shaming the summer sun in monarch fire
bringing, as the Victorians said,
their passion, creativity—
sometimes grief, but not
this time.
Expectations irrational?
(if perfect)

the petunias tumble their velvet petals
Our guitars chime
We are the poets in the bathtub
with fewer bones on display
our mature bellies
glutted with music and ecstasy

Vandal 13

This wad of susceptible clay,
chewed gum,
formed vulnerable
to vocals like these

to a puzzle
so bold
though vulnerable, too
—and more so.

Where else could I go?

Vandal 14

The stories I could TELL when we all trade news —
too much of a stir, too intense the stirring
for one too plain and prone to laughter

the stories
I could tell you,
my romance-craving
fellow library-chicks

though not succinctly.

...

Vandal 15

One excruciating summer—
but would I tell the grandchildren?
Will there be grandchildren?

Tomorrow a birthday party
and then no backdoor to this parlor…..
too many in a ridiculously handsome
and artistic family
in which to stir enmity

too many of his
golden-hearted allies
scattered about town.

Noodles, all, my muscles of Acceptance.

I refused to accept
What Is

(empty)
(failure to beguile,
to connect, failure to fairytale)

and for survival,
disengaged.
I built my carapace
segment by segment
barring the door against tortures
particular to my wiring.

Hey.
To backpedal now
would be to unravel
years of labor.

I pedal forward

we wait out the summer
in ludicrous sweat
We continue in occasional bodily entanglements
followed by long discussions of
theology, philosophy, divorce, diseases of delusion
and the Desert Fathers.

...

I vow to myself to practice
practice
practice
Acceptance
the ideal accessory to one
with so spidering a shell
as mine.

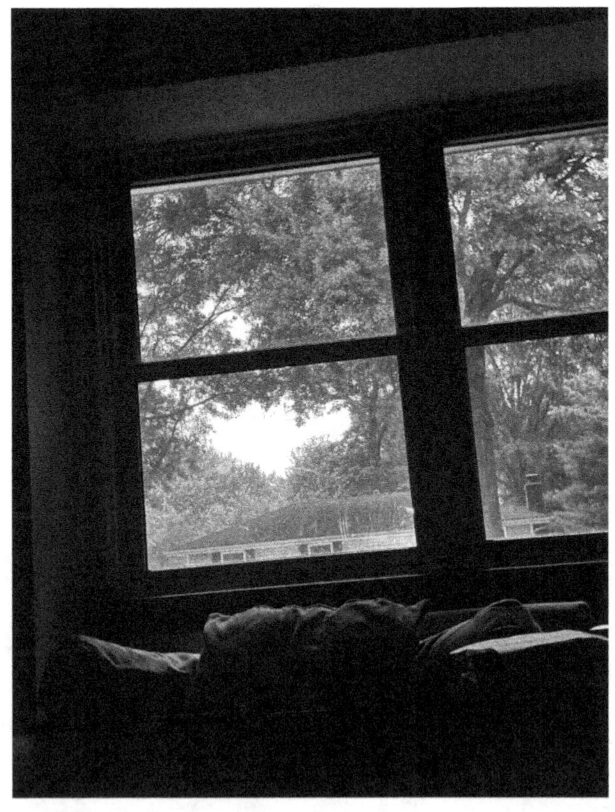

Damn *that* one
in his blue-eyed magnetism.
Damn his singular tunes.

I practice radical acceptance
of the major poets
and photorealistic artists
he has known.

I boldly imbibe—no, chug—
the reality
of his
his

knowledge

his deep and
deep-pressed knowledge
of any female acquaintance
into whom we might bump.

The comments on posts:
"We should catch up."

what have you done, lurid one?

What are you doing,
cracked egg?
Close your chicken-eyes.
stand tiptoe on slimy cliff
at the verge of the pounding sea
breathing the salt-fish air

...

until turned inside-out
vanished
secluded
in the far and mighty
above it all.

But first
go on I must cry
only slightly.

mourn what I missed
and memories he cherishes

mourn bitterness of
loving too intensely
invisibly
all too visibly

cast aside by prospective
employers

sic these thoughts on a blessing
descend on it, obliterate it
as bugs
on a corpse.
Oh how you grieve.
You shouldn't
have thrown her away…

Love too deep
cursed by the devils
to this plagued route

...

leave me be
alone in my haunted forest
with the wolves,
werewolves,
dizzying herbs
And hidden creatures

Clear is the abandon
I must choose
or burn all
within my meager radius.

Sprawled
diagonal across the bed
you crowd and take

I contract
and shrivel
in accordance
At some point
I must matter.

And you, the new,
curling around me
intuitive straitjacket
adapting and molding,
squeezing adoration
into my bones and veins
merging, osmotic:

when we catalogued our neuroses
you warned me of
your maudlin times to come.

...

[Song]
Nicotine Headache

Your nicotine headache is mine
—it belongs to me
I could stay out here all night
in the gloaming
June is halfway over
—oh my god it's still June
——-and gone, the strawberry moon

I sense I'm being prepared for solitude or death
Moon flowers love me with their cleansing breath
Bright star, audacious, sing your fire to me
Thrill me, Nightingale, but only sparingly….

From last Wolf Moon to the next Wolf Moon
We build our sweet Brigadoon

Drop the cigarette and let me taste your teeth
No regrets–castanets–in a smoky wreath
Thrill me, Nightingale, with your crushing tune— mouths gush with berries
Every strawberry moon
Gush—every–strawberry mooooooooooooon.

22 years:
a fair run
for one
who finds his partner
an easy presence in the room
her laughter secret gemstones
clanging in the breeze

and for the clanging laugher
pinched in a ball
levitating nervous in the booth
alone at IHOP
dropping tears for the kindness of the waitress
in merely bringing the coffee
and leaving the jug
knowing she is there,
levitating.

(what will happen
if I unclench?)

(how madly will the universe careen?)

(that is what she used to say)

...

Remember, pines, when it was only us?
I came to cry in silence.
You wrapped me in your breath
of calming, cooling purity
and I knew that you knew me
running to you
just to be.

Jackie Davis whirled on a Hammond organ
a cyclone of mirth and swell
back-when
in swell post-war days when skirts were postwar
abundant and in the car, driving to church,
three-quarters of a century later
we danced with our arms, shoulders
eyes and teeth,
cha-cha wrists ~ ballet fingertips ~
golden smiles -
grinding imaginary sausage
in the front seats
mortifying our teenaged child
and taxing his sensory integration through the backseat speaker.

"He's going to be so confused," said you,
imagining the dialogue:
"'You guys were getting along so well!
Whahoppened?'"

"The pressure was off, that's what," I offered, lame
in useless truth.

...

A different Jackie Davis,
not the lively organist,
fervent. joyous—
but a different Jackie Davis
used to live down the street
back-when
there, big house on the corner,
in days the tornado hit your
Sedalia bedroom
and your wide eyes aged five
couldn't comprehend why you
had to clean up the mess
when the tornado did it.
(three more, even younger.
that is probably why,
or maybe your memory of memory
leaned severe)

The other Jackie Davis was in
junior high when I was five or six
and you were seven or eight
and I saw him only in blitz of strides
tall and pewter-blond, mythical,
otherworldly,
keeping his music in secret.

Your songs, yours,
filled the car and you sang of me,
the invisible,
as possessed by angels
as burning light
as better, inspiring, and
damn the world.
As brightly visible, nearly blinding.
And so
where else could I go?

...

oh thank you,
I didn't ruin everything yet
when my kid called—-

I stayed overlong
with a lover's head in my lap
a shimmering cordial, that,
and too many cigarettes
—- and i would not tell him where I was
when he asked four times, just curious
and I played it off as being a Woman of Mystery
and brought him the requested cheeseburger

("sus" he had texted, following a photographed
box of Choco Chimps,
amusing breakfast cereal—
he won't touch the stuff but being
a paragon of his generation's
surreal and unexpected humor
enjoys photographing the amusing brands)

But I had bought a pile
of 50-cent composition books
at Walmart,
the last stand at that price
and oh god my web of lies-by-omission

I fled to the drive-thrus,
forgetting my phone
on my lover's balcony

How tenderly you opened the door
when I knocked—
having fled the drive-thrus
to retrieve my phone
from your elysian balcony
where you told me scenes
from Henry V
while I smoked.

How tenderly I dig my hole
in anticipation of the songs we'll sing,
of our cornbread nights come autumn

Our time spent filled my being and belly
as your head filled my lap
Dear God!
Too much blessing!
How else is there to see it?
Am i cracked?
How luxuriously cracked i am
and just happy to be here. There.
Entwined.

...

Attempts to picture my life with you
Always touch down in your apartment
instead of my modest, sunny little
1978 tri-level house with the original
Kitchen linoleum.
Your dim, gold lighting enfolds me.
Yours alone, and the things you own.
Your festival of books on top of books.

One shelf collapsed in the bedroom
while you worked at the kitchen table,
listening to music.

The shelf would have landed on your head,
you said, if I had not lent you that portable
record player when the other went mute,
and I was your guardian angel that night.

We are mist
Created for relationship

I am mist

"God jealously longs for the spirit he has caused to dwell in us"
jealousy
only once have I inspired jealousy
Twice? Is that relevant?

God is in love with us
forgives and befriends "Humble yourself before the Lord
and he will lift you up"

acknowledge your arrogance, poet ~ the lynchpin of the universe
is not you

(this is anti-poet.
humility is poetry's opposite.)

Humility—I have misplaced your phone number.
my desires. mine.
Humility—humiliation—you have been my constant companion and
now I have slammed the door on you
in a storm

I boast of my arrogant schemes.
This is evil.

Is this unbridled pride?
Was I dying of thirst?
God opposes me…?

…

If I fall on my knees in humility
will I continue forward in my agenda?

We are of mist
and God is forever
The closer I draw near to God
(in my love of the calendula) (in adoration of Your music)
(in sunrise elation and full-moon bath)
(in fireside, story, and song)

the nearer to me is my God
Relevant … Revenant
Temptation
to spend my days reading and writing of revenants

as opposed to pondering what is sin
what is self-centered
and what is a fond, forgiving human farewell and onward.

Lover,
I love your love of story

and the laundry in a heap on the bed
getting more and more wrinkled as my mother's ghost
becomes more and more rankled

Weird, Weird Summer

Alternate title: "Song 5 a.m."

123. over
here only loosely stitched in some ways
in other ways, seamless—so together
i park my mind on a melon rind
because it's summer
i'll never be right again

Ref:
weird, weird summer
smoke too much
turn the whole world inside-out & such
freaked-out solstice scrub the floor
and thrash guitar and thrash some more
verse? bridge?
how clean are you?
how mean are you?
Not too shabby—a little bit crabby
how green today?
how obscene today?
coyotes hysterical—take me away

weird weird summer
not a pool in sight
emotional corset laced too tight
wiggy hot spell
make a mean cole slaw
then duck a visit to your mother-in-law

...

(verse, chanted)
yoga time, sunny jane
loosen those hips
loosen that mind
sink a dozen ships
and which of your seven clothes will you wear?
and what the gum drops will you do with your hair?

weird weird summer
now pitch the tent and light the fire
your mind is bent
weirdo summer
on spongy ground
amok, all slavering, upside-down
fun house, madhouse, a wild sock hop
I just gotta see my sweet gum drop (x3)

just a person nothing more just a person nothing more just a person nothing more leave the gum drops on the floor on the floor on the floor on the floor floor floor floor flooorrrrt

I cry for the nine wasps I killed,
their corpses sprawled on the porch concrete
where I smoke my Lucky Strike,
the heavy Reds that buzz me,
turning my tears to stupor—
my tears for you
and for the love you couldn't demonstrate,
as you learned at your mother's knee.

She is the center of the universe,
as far as I can see.
She instructs God
and he obeys.

You are
a
worthwhile
human being,
my friend—

no matter how tight
her fist,
however alien
and ludicrous her indifference.

Our neighbor owl
swoops into the pines.

You
are
seen.

...

Cigarettes:

Thursday: 3 ~ rage at current in-laws
Friday: 2 ~ rage diminished; cooled but pulsing
Saturday: 2 ~ post-work glorious summer evening with blackberry wine and absence of smoking-hot nicotine pal
Sunday: 4 ½ ~ balcony time with nicotine friend
(who smokes in halves)
(who waters the Dragon Sunset plants and returns to his seat, takes a cigarette and lights it, all in a fluid motion — stares and swears at the cigarette in his silky-smooth left hand, confused at its sudden materiality)
~ postponement of marriage or you're a terrible mother
~ all of his other women were silky-smooth. Not a Hot Sasquatch like me among them.
~ Job hunt age 48, careerless & hirsute poet, overly abundant input from many white males ~ have you overdrawn your courage, Hot Sasquatch? Weren't you a force once? Sort of?
-Hear this:
They are powerless to poison you, Luscious Polish Peasant of the Glimmering Leg Hair. Refuse to be poisoned.
~ The curls of thin smoke were lace alive and dancing.

Cigarettes, 2

Monday: 1 ~ I should be doing any number of other things:
~throwing clay
~learning my song about the naked ghost
~planning hippie dinners for a week of strong poetry
~reading Jack Kerouac's reprint of traveling tales
~brewing the vanilla tea
~yoga for nicotine headaches
~clearing the bathroom for renovation
~harvesting medicinal marigolds
~organizing the coffee cabinet
~drowning in vinegar the bugs that eat the blackberry leaves
~but god I miss him.

Tuesday: 1 ~ for no good reason
("Well, it's not good… but it's a reason."
~ Bing Crosby, Danny Kaye)

Wednesday: 1 ~ for displacement amid bathroom renovation ~ for one's lover still asleep at his place
~ it fell out of the car ashtray in the Denny's parking lot and a mad search ensued. (floorboard under driver's seat, smoldering.)
~ I stub it out. By now, I have misplaced the lighter. A comedy of errors ensues.
~ oh right. it's a 2005 Subaru Outback. The car is equipped with a cigarette lighter. I always forget.
~ there might be more. I am seeing him today.
…..
~ the 5th cigarette blurred the moon.

...

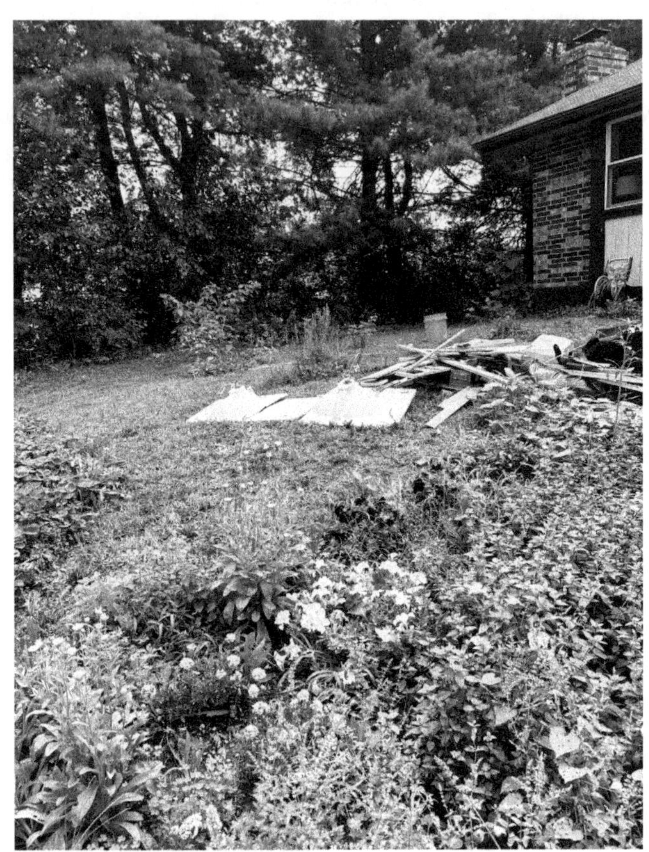

Childhood sinks facedown in the garden!

One foot in the afterlife
and cannot, would not escape it,
loved as I am there.

What would be the point of
luxuriating at home today,
aside from this
malicious rainstorm?

No hope in it, ever,
until I stay alone.

"Alone!" once my songbeam,
concocting solo Christmases
awash in innovative wassails!

—certain, bone-deep, that my destiny was the flipside—
doomed, abandoned due to
Flaring Insanity

and hark to the new happy couple,
poolside shaking their sideways heads:

hmm. Such a shame she
could never get her shit together Tsk….

but… I told myself:
alone is better

with no innocents
to absorb my shrapnel…

There might be shrapnel,

...

I sense it already, it lurks
in the mists,
zooming toward the slight relaxing
of his admittedly hectic initial pursuit

and dismissing the dramatic blooms
of his courtesy,
guessing just to one side
at the cause of my discomfort
but always sensing it,
radiant of soul.

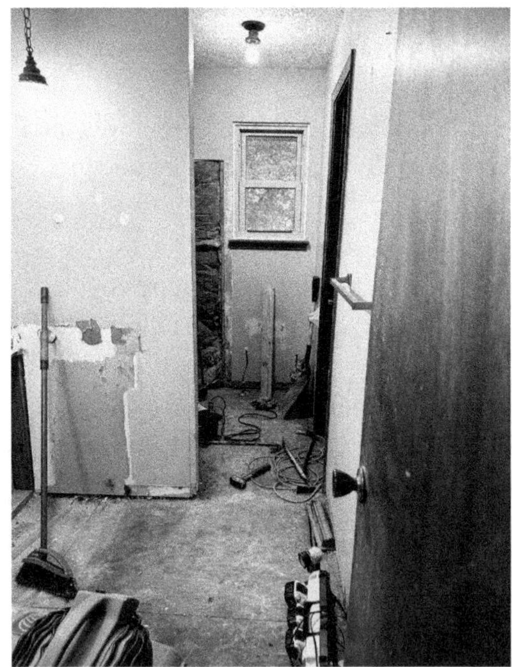

Bathroom guts

Yesterday you said

and I went on about the smooth-legged girls
confessed to shaving my legs since the age of nine
and no longer interested in such pursuits
as short on reward as that

we should not get married until November

and I savored the cigarette
stared at the chimneys
relished your eyes like a drunken nymph to be pitied.

not the upcoming November
but the one after that

these things always begin
with furious quoting of lines
from Raising Arizona…

That is the only way to be the right kind of mother.

He's right.
He's right.

I make a remark that reminds you of a line of my poetry
and you quote it to me, smiling.

he was not the type of son that his father expected and his father could not stop worrying about it, back then…

Also you love this apartment and want time before it goes away.

...

I should tell the story of the cocktail,
the Satan's Whisker
from the Agatha Christie play
but no ingress presents itself...
and the scene is pleasant to me

You do not want to get married until the November after next.
That caught up to me a day later.

But always sensing it,
radiant soul.

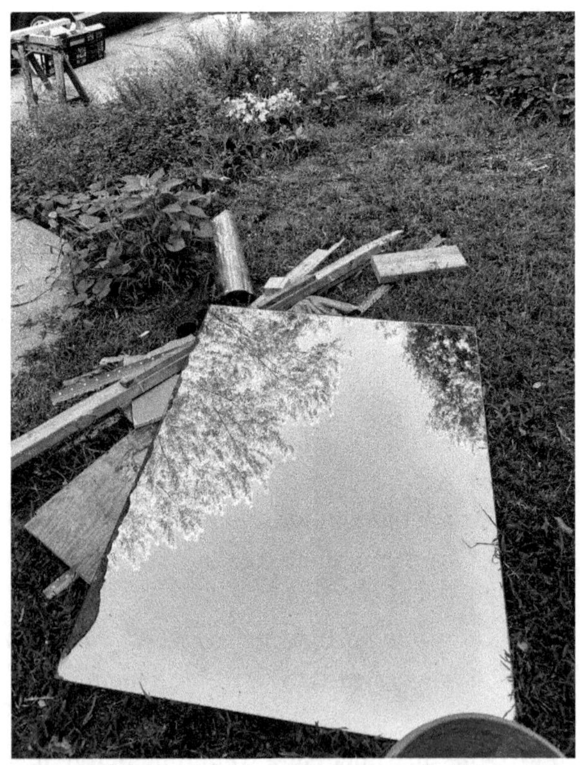

Childhood bathroom mirror full of sky

Cigarettes, 3

Thursday ~ 0
(work)
(his illness)

Friday ~ 3
(in the car after a trip to his school-year cigarette haunt, run by a doting Middle Eastern widow and her nephew) ~ (she remembered him, doted, glowed at me when he said I would be his wife one day)
(in the sweaty evening, leaning on the hood of his car after his folk-punk band was the featured group at the prestigious open mic night)
(and another, late, on the balcony)

Saturday ~ 3?
How can I recall it?
(one after visiting Scout Camp ~ entanglement, long tradition, ceremonial names and otherwise)
(one—again—but when? Again on the balcony, evening, after the transcendent meatloaf he made with Cheez-its and barbecue sauce)
(one amid the weird dope-trip, which made no sense at all)

Sunday ~ 1
(he joined his church)

Tuesday ~ not 1 but 3
(how much longer will I work at this library?)
(job interview)
(this glorious balcony)

…

FLOWER.

I believe you've been rendered speechless, my dear
~ he said ~ no, really ~ perhaps ~ almost surely ~
as I gaped at the weird streetlight of unshielded filaments
and concentrated dearly to keep my soul close by.

Don't let me fly away
Don't let me fly away
I repeat in distant whispers
and it's a glowing gospel anthem
with mellotrons and sweat and breath
and Truth
don't ~~~ let ~~~ me
flye awaye…………

I whistle for my soul around corners
behind gravestones
and it fades, recedes,
here is the map on the study door
and here is the bookcase
then the swallowing dim
back and forth and round she goes.
If I can't find the map again,
lighted, bright-eyed,
then I will be dead soon.

The chattering music hushes from the walls
and dawn bowls in a little weird still
but I drive anyway to feed the cat
and there is no skipping church,
not today, the day he joins
and his parents, still living, accompany us

His late-night laughter fizzed and anchored me
but he couldn't stay near,
too high, too hungry for cigarettes
while I clung to life on earth in the blankets

and in the leaden glow of morning
I lay touchless.

Midnight Cigarette

Does this one count as one of Wednesday's five
or the first of Thursday's mystery number?

(assisting him as he cuts buck)
(I must buy him more of these
expensive ones i've smoked too many)
(must return to the roses)
(this glorious balcony)
(soon to resume my other life, weirdly)

I slept too late and napped too long,
wanting him near me.

Whisky and cigarette
midnight and I see Mars blinking
All that is missing is the marshmallow.

Lord, meet me here.

In sugar and smoke I ruin me.

Look to the trees
and the bats and fireflies
of a steamy porch twilight.

Life is well underway.
know that
in the last hurrah
of a whiskey sour.

Today my longing was 2 ½ cigarettes in scope.

...

I'll never tell him
that his gut reacted to yogurt
in the same way
as his rival's
and how they share philosophies
down to identical phrasing
Regarding …
what it was I can't recall.

It was weeks ago,
and too, too spooky.
Or that each wanted the same
gold-lipped, folk-guitar-goddess
photograph of me,
never photographed, a screenshot
from a film I made myself.

But I won't tell them
of their uncanny parallels.

They need never know.

I am stronger. dammit, than the letter I wrote.
I have no need of anyone
and look gleefully forward
to my lone-wolf days.
Your coughs are all lost to the cosmos.
I wallow in kale and lentils,
offending no one.
Pointless, this temptation to cry.

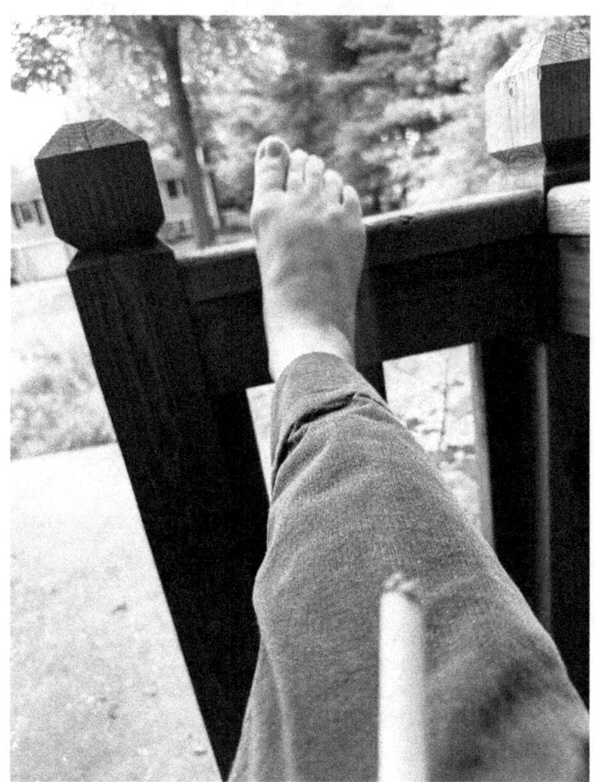

Porch Smoke

...

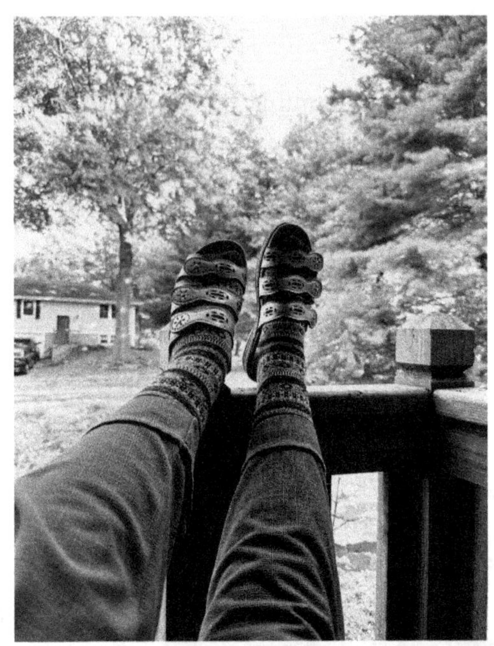

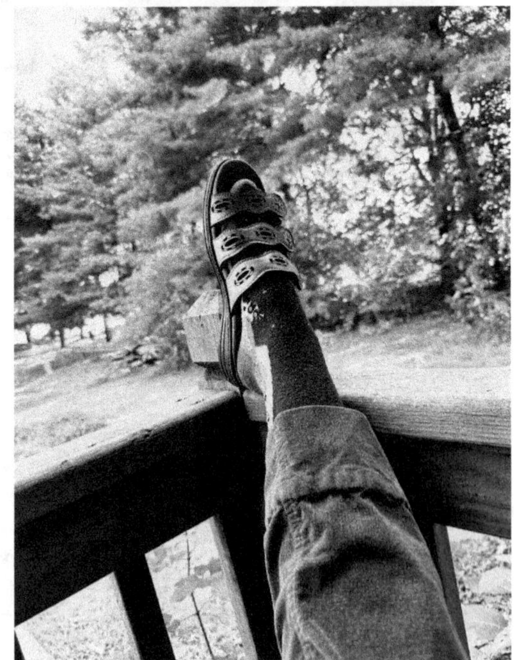

Socks & Sandals ~ Vandal!

Smoke Porch Playlist ...

In Spite of All the Danger ~ from the *Nowhere Boy* soundtrack
Jenny Artichoke ~ Kaleidoscope
The Rat's Revenge ~ The Rats
Trickle Trickle ~ The Videos
I Make the Love ~ Ronnie Dawson
The One ~ The Lemon Twigs
This Ain't a Good Time ~ Big Sandy and His Fly-Rite Boys
The Truth Often Hurts the Heart ~ Chad & Jeremy
Radar Love ~ Bob's Burgers
Why Should I Care ~ Chad & Jeremy
As Tears Go By ~ Marianne Faithfull
I Have Dreamed ~ Chad & Jeremy
Say it Isn't True ~ Chad & Jeremy
Donna, Donna ~ Chad & Jeremy
Dream a Little Dream of Me ~ The Mamas and the Papas
Someday ~ Cracker
Pictures of Matchstick Men ~ Camper Van Beethoven
Love is All Around ~ The Troggs

...

porch lights grow searchlights
through my lashes when i wink

he fled and groaned when we told him
and overturned an upstairs loveseat
and emptied a bookshelf
then set it back right shortly after
today:
my fever and three cigarettes
washed the dishes
and put clean sheets on the bed

I didn't pick the raspberries
and the calendula withered on my watch
oh criminy
o criminal
Ruinator
Ruminating

Immunity tea and cigarette breakfast
Sweet moonflower blooms
made the cat sneeze like a man

in crosswise clangor
to the man who sneezes like
a big, tough kitten.

...

But was it?
All for him?

Marriage depleted
with the love starved out of me
over a decade
of piteous pining for a smile,
for a hand held…

Ruminate ruminate.
Ruinate.

Self Overdose.

Tobacco-perfumed hands
splayed
on the yoga mat at sunrise.

goddess belly yearns and sings
in vigorous youth.

Nebulous truth.

The tea dust in the cup
spells chaos
winding weird like gentle smoke.

"Hey, go look at the moon,"
I told you, having phoned
two minutes after our parting.
"It will explain everything about today."

"Okay, I'll go do it!"
you agreed, eyes dancing audibly.

Mother worked for the phone company
35 years and insisted
she always knew
when the moon was full
—broad daylight, no windows —
she knew
by the unhinged nature of the public
"getting drunk and
playing on the telephone,"
as she summed it.

Now on the eve of the Blue Supermoon,
working at a grade-school,
everyone felt it.

"Hey, did everyone feel it today?"
I asked the teachers as I nearly galloped
to my car.

Oh, they did. Oh, you did.
And I did

in my creeping phobias
my distrust of technology and my all-too-newness
at yet another new job

…

this one an alien planet,
so bombastically systemic,
fully permeated and beloved.
A cult

jealously guarding its insights
cloaked in lingo and
inscrutable abbreviations and accesses withheld.

As moon-tuned poet -slash-
occasional substitute teacher
what a grandiose fraud,
telling the children
to sit quietly and fill in worksheets
when they should be under the sky,
faces buried in sunbeams and honeysuckle.

As sporadic keeper of the outlaws—
I get it.

O pure morning air
and birdsongs embroidering among
whatever else comes today

I cherish this cigarette
as another jeweled peg in my being.

"Have as many experiences as you can
in this life," he said
—may he live to be my next
father-in-law.
He raised a hand to touch mine
twice
in greeting and farewell
at the party last night.

My Lord, Christ,
be near me every minute.
My Father in Heaven,
oh Your precious numberless mercies.

Inform my every breath today
however flawed
and let the children come to me
and find kindness anyway.

...

My hilarious child
sums up my job:

"I'm a superstar!"
(gravelly voice)
"I might have farted in my teacher's face,
but now I get to play with

SAND!"

Hysterically accurate.

This is the night when
I am the worst villain I know.

The terse is deafening
the silence bombastic

oh
God
for a train
whistle

to go with this whiskey.

...

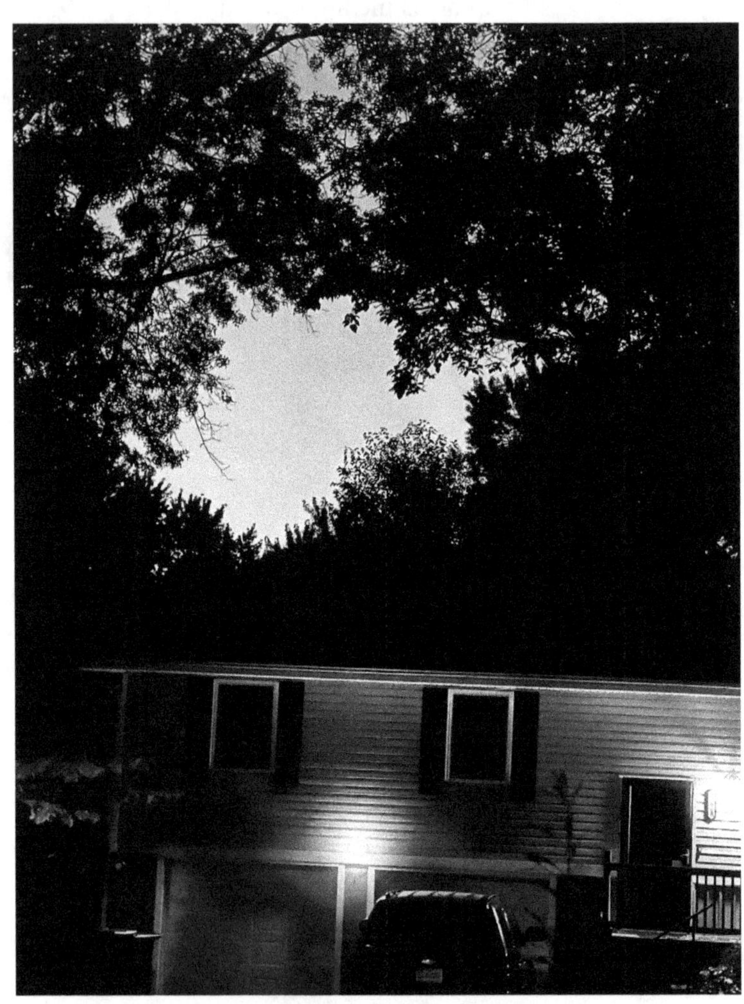

Warped-heart hole in the trees

Alone with the last cigarette
and the warped-heart hole in the trees.

Shave your legs and armpits.

But to avoid this
is part of who I am.

Cramming the self into
numbers of molds
is my task now

after locating my ways at long last
and championing blissful acceptance
of my only self's reality
and the creation
of one's own rules

Descended of peasants
both Polish and English
And I am far from smooth.
Miles from airbrushed flawless
And?

this might be the whisky talking
but you:
you bone-delight in your solitude
you treasure your gaming groups
your expansive family
and your music
and your writing

...

where is my crevice?
  where is my place of
    … of…?

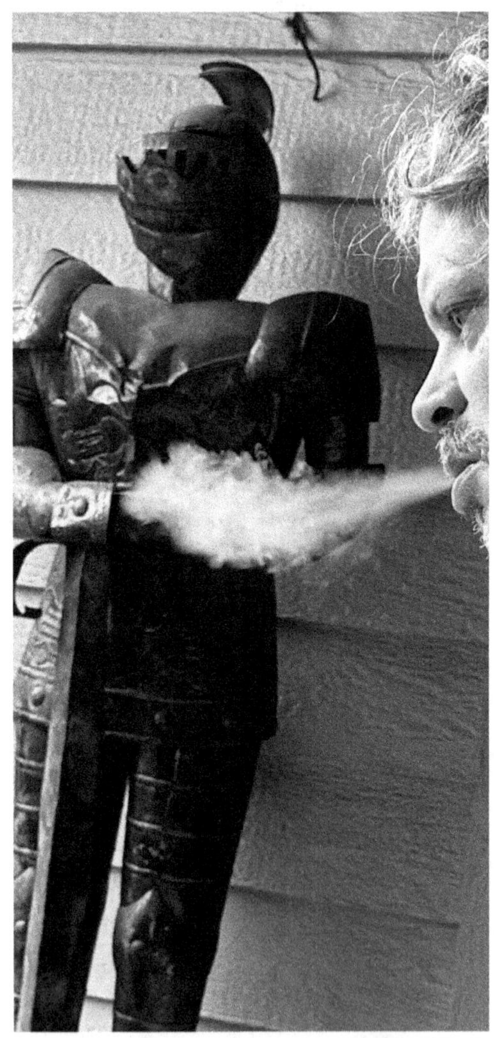

Delirious, rich and anguished this dysregulation
and I cling to the spinning of it
the thrill and the colors

Hello my songs of insanity
hello
and be you woven among my veins
for now at least
and let the emeralds rain down

A calming approaches but I shun it
bathed in bourbon
resting numbed
and gutting You my Maker

no ~

and evoking in You ~
eliciting
Your caring adoration
my Maker.

...

(drunk text)

Yesterday 10:59 PM

hey listen
it is certainly the whisky talking
but my leg hair is GODDESS

my armpit hair is ANGELS

in dust of diamonds my lamb

I will ponder that as I make fish sticks, heh. Because I am making a late dinner. Nicotine headache but I should have seen that coming.

oops poor baby

(with Seann)

He's always had a thing about the clock.
7:14
Hey look, it's our wedding anniversary!
9:17
Hey look, it's your birthday!
The trees in the front yard
teased out my tears this morning.
My poet-friend reminded me
that I am a poet
(in spite of the institution that employs me).

The time is 7:14 a.m.
Am I wicked, Lord?
I am meant to be small
and it is entirely possible
that I am one of the wicked
sung and shunned in the Psalms

but thank you for hearing
my prayers of the morning.

...

Today I made stew
chopped up the goods
and stirred in the meat
and all
and put it in the oven
for five hours

and broadcasted poetry
using old poems
about the opposites
of poetry.

There.
All clear to chill now.
Permission given.

I smoke one more
to love him more subtly,
to lessen my fever—
to hush, impossibly blithe,
my shouting adoration
too thoroughly sparked
in birthday glow
in rogue-wave ecstasy.

words of treasured poets
markered in his own sure
and lightning hand
on walls of a wooden crate

filled with encouragement
And tribute for my song.

He cradles my heart
and loves me
with his entirety.

...

I thought about eating a moonflower
on the night you were still sick.
Their hallucinations bloom generous,
it's said, but also
Their threat of comas.

The high-end blender growled
Through grinding of sliced ginger
And oranges and lemons
To your health

but I didn't bring them
and it tore at my essence,
grated it fine. ailing.

The plunger of the french press
pinned the garlic and thyme,
soaking for tea
to your health

but my child knew
it was for you
and hid the mixtures
and I stepped back
and did not interfere.

he spent the week
hating me in secret
loudly to his confidant

and finally would not yield
in his disdain
of your health

In his healing pleasure
of wounding,
shattered lamb,
wounded.

...

22 years ago
our landlord was Russian,
walking us through our newly
fixed-up apartment
with his beautifully
sleepy-eyed daughter, Ellen,
a new mother.

Crossing the threshold
he spoke to her in soft Russian
and she returned a groggy
Russian half-sentence,
weighted with baby carrier,
then
waved a gentle hand,
"I'll deal with you later"

and today I am she

crossing thresholds of
misunderstanding
and ill communication
a newly despised old mother
a vandal
a fuck-up
wading through my
tenderly cultivated messes

climbing over the bodies
oh my three wounded ones

and flutter my digits.

I'll deal with you
later.

...

[Poet Problems]

thought, cool, I can go! but oh my crap they're the opening band and he's my ride--parking is a nightmare--so he has to get there at like 6 and it's rude not to stay for their friend-band afterward so ---11:30 we're all done? I MIGHT DIE. 😂

These all sound like dramatic, glitter dipped poet problems to have... 😆

TRUE!!! How are you doing?

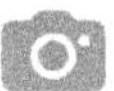
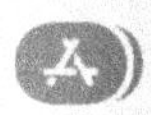
Text Message

Abbreviated poet problems with Angela Yuriko Smith

I told you
  I would
fuck this up.

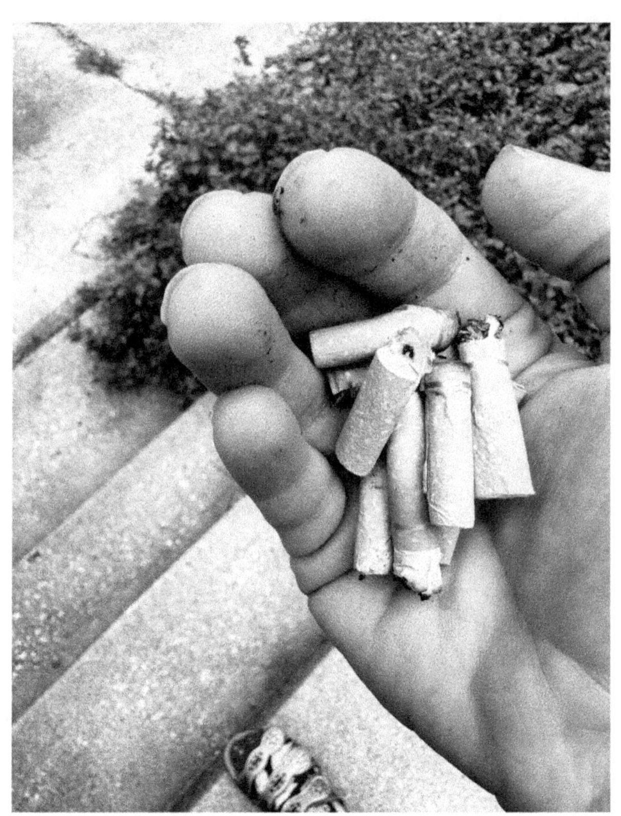

...

Even the moon hides her eyes
in tree limbs
swallowing her puke
as I look upon the wreckage
of my selfish devotion.

My deeds reject the child
my only child
my one necessity
my one.

My one who lived inside of me
sleeping by day as I worked
walking the public library
rocking him

terrifying me with his
stillness one day off.

My one
whom my body
nourished and cradled.

I am a piece of shit
and no longer his mother
he says.
I have left him behind.

But will I?
Will time soften him?

“That which you long for
is not for you,”
Life has said
many times
of various desires

and says so again.
Tonight. This night
as I breathe
by stifled moonlight.

Adoration.
To adore
and be adored
palpably

is not mine.

Is not to be mine
if I want to remain a mother.

...

Dearest angel.
Blue-eyed.
A smoldering 51.
Spiced and precious.

Today the fireworks emerged from the storm clouds
(fully clothed).

What will I do with you
at day's end?

What of your shining comforts?
What of your cheek
resting on the top of my head
as you clasp me
enamored
in wide open spaces?

What
will I do about you?

Moon surfaces
approving of my agony.

Tonight I was you,
angel pie,
in my chain-smoking stupor.

Tonight I was me
in my whisky bath.

Six End Tables
(song)

he took six out of six end tables
there's a futon where the bed once sat
six out of six end tables
and i'm really gonna miss the cat

ok, he took only four end tables
and he left the ugly ones for me
alone in a dearth of heartbeats
and i really really miss the kitty
Am G Am
that night i ate one cookie
Am C E
and too much candy corn
Am C Am
had coffee, cigarettes and whisky
G E Am
and settled into being reborn
Bridge
Dm C Am
all the good headphones are gone
(i'll have to buy some)
Dm C Am
i watch whatever i want
(on the tv)
Am C Dm
only cheap whisky on the premises E Am
that's who i am that's who i am…
Verse

...

i got two out of six end tables
and i baked a cake of course
22 years ain't a bad try
oh man, what a friendly divorce
a friendly divorce, what a guy
22 years ain't a bad try
i want too much from my life
hello suitors beware
i can't remember your name lee ingleby
i can't remember my name
mizfrantic swaddle me in smoke and flame
little lucky strike
life won't ever be the same
hallelujah white pines shiver with grace
sweet medicine moonflowers cover the place
in the morning
ba-bomp ba-da-da da
bomp badada daaaaa

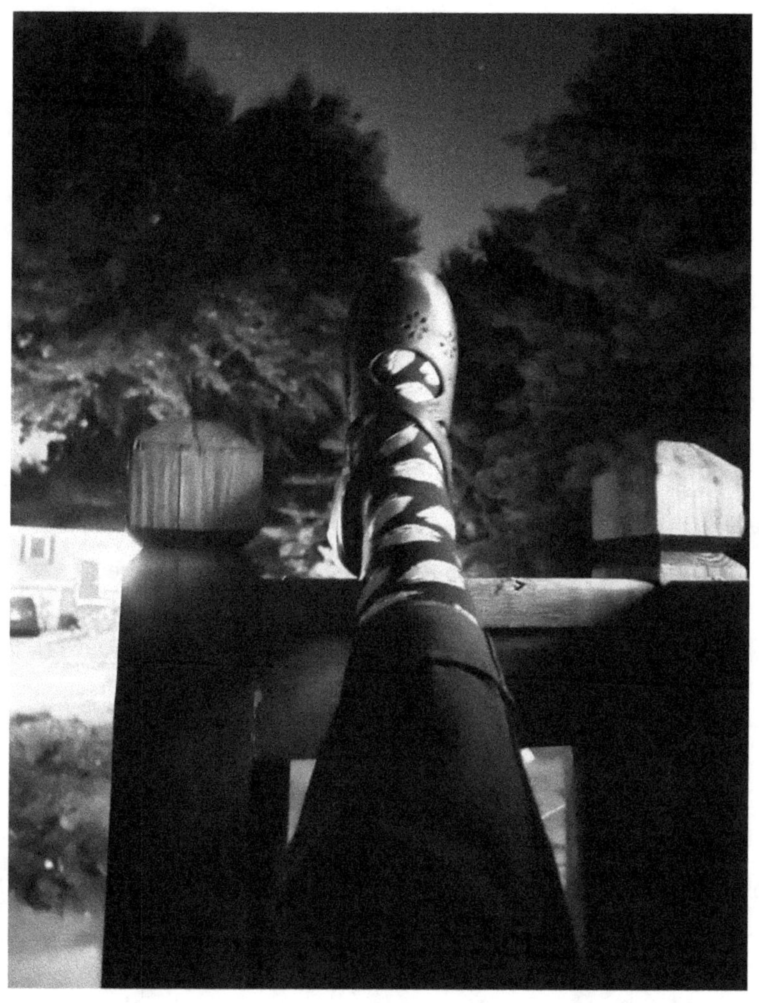

...

Vandal Playlist

Somerset Gloucestershire Wassail ~ Kingston Trio
Mary Mild ~ Kingston Trio
The Boar's Head Carol ~ Magpie Lane
May Song ~ Magpie Lane
Green Green ~ The New Christy Minstrels
Hi Jolly ~ The New Christy Minstrels
My Dear Mary Anne ~ The New Christy Minstrels
Ride, Ride, Ride ~ The New Christy Minstrels
A Travelin' Man ~ The New Christy Minstrels
The Three Ravens ~ The Black Country Three
Catch the Wind ~ Donovan
I'll Never Find Another You ~ The Seekers
The Last Thing on My Mind ~ The Seekers
A World of Our Own ~ The Seekers
Atlantis ~ Donovan
Heaven is Being With You ~ Jackie DeShannon

Oh my god that is such blissfully square medicine.

https://youtube.com/playlist?list=PL8eYqPatH7nTBOqdK-e5dMXBb1wb-V9CeB&si=ls7fd1OZeXip8ouk

www.ingramcontent.com/pod-product-compliance
Lightning Source LLC
LaVergne TN
LVHW010940110826
845149LV00013B/2684

* 9 7 8 1 9 5 9 0 4 8 1 1 4 *